LESLEY RILEY

create with
Transfer Artist Paper

15 projects for crafters, quilters, mixed media & fine artists

C&T PUBLISHING

ext and photography copyright © 2011 by Lesley Riley

Photography and artwork Copyright © 2011 by C&T Publishing, Inc.

Publisher: Amy Marson

Creative Director: Gailen Runge

Acquisitions Editor: Susanne Woods

Editor: Lynn Koolish

Technical Editor: Helen Frost

Copyeditor/Proofreader: Wordfirm Inc.

Cover Designer: Kristen Yenche

Book Designer: Kerry Graham

Production Coordinator: Jenny Leicester

Production Editor: Julia Cianci

Photography by Christina Carty-Francis and Diane Pedersen
of C&T Publishing, Inc., unless otherwise noted

Published by C&T Publishing, Inc., P.O. Box 1456, Lafayette, CA 94549

Library of Congress Cataloging-in-Publication Data

Riley, Lesley (Lesley Jackson), 1952-

 Create with Transfer Artist Paper : Use TAP To Transfer Any Image
onto Fabric, Paper, Wood, Glass, Metal, Clay & More! / Lesley Riley.

    pages cm

 ISBN 978-1-60705-267-8 (soft cover)

 1. Handicraft. 2. Transfer-printing. 3. Iron-on transfers. I. Title.

 TT880.R55 2011

 745.5--dc22

                    2010048435

Printed in China

10 9 8 7 6 5 4 3 2

Contents

Dedication

Hey, reader—this book is dedicated to you! Yes, you. I wrote this book for you. If we're lucky, we have already met. If not, hopefully we will meet somewhere, someday. If our paths do cross, please stop me and say hello. And if it so happens that our paths never cross, I am happy just knowing that I have done my small part in inspiring you to create. You see, all I've ever wanted to do was to create art that inspires others the way that so many artists have inspired me, made me smile, and made my life a little better by sharing themselves and their art with the world. If you are reading this book, then I've done what I set out to do. Thank you for being a part of my journey.

Acknowledgments

It has again been a pleasure to work with the wonderful team at C&T. Lynn Koolish's gentle persistence is what put this book in your hands, and her editorial eye helped to make it the resource that it is. Thanks to Mary Wruck and Amy Marson for seeing the possibilities in TAP (Transfer Artist Paper) and making the decision to sell TAP under the C&T name. That made it possible for me to take off my TAP shoes and continue my dance with life.

I want to thank the amazing group that turns a book into a reality and then tells the world about it:

Christina Carty-Francis and Diane Pederson for the art of the photo

Helen Frost for her eagle-eye editing

Kristen Yenche and Kerry Graham for turning text and photos into a work of art

Jenny Leicester and Julia Cianci for keeping the book on track

Lisa Fulmer for being such an amazing TAP dance partner

Introduction

Transfer Artist Paper, TAP for short, is an iron-on transfer paper. It was developed for fabric transfers. But like any artist, I wondered first, "What else will it work on?" I am happy to report the answer: "Lots of things."

In this book I share everything I know about TAP. But as with any new product in the hands of artists like you, new ideas and discoveries are being made every day. While TAP was designed for transferring images and artwork onto fabric, in my quest to find the perfect, multisurface transfer method, I put TAP to the test on some of the most common quilting, collage, and mixed-media surfaces. I was ecstatic over what TAP could do. TAP is as close to a perfect method as I have found in my 30+ years of transferring.

If you are new to transfers, you probably have many questions. If you are familiar with many or most of the transfer methods, you may be wondering why I think TAP is tops, so much so that I'm willing to stake my name and reputation on it.

In the pages that follow, you will discover what I found to be the pros and cons of TAPping onto various surfaces, as well as specific directions and in-depth information about each surface. There are also 15 projects to get you started, and the examples throughout will serve as inspiration as well.

And there's one last thing before you get to all the juicy details—don't forget to add that one necessary ingredient to your TAPping—your imagination. Don't take what I have to say as the *only* ways to use TAP. Most of what I discovered about TAP's possibilities is a result of asking, "What if …?" I've tried to tell you everything I know about TAP. If something comes to mind that I haven't covered, then try it out for yourself. Experiment. You have nothing to lose but your uncertainty. And remember this: If at first you don't succeed, try again. Things don't always work the first time you try anything, so try again. Consider this book your invitation to the dance, the TAP dance. Once you get a feel for TAP, or as I like to say, get your TAP shoes on, I hope you will join the show and share your discoveries and projects with us. Visit us online at http://www.flickr.com/groups/happytappers/.

All about TAP

What Is TAP?

TAP (Transfer Artist Paper) is a specially designed paper that is sprayed with a polymer coating. This coating is designed to accept inkjet printer inks and other art materials, such as markers, crayons, charcoal, pastels, paints, pens, and inks. It does not work with laser toner.

When the coating is heated with an iron or heat press, it combines with the printer ink or art materials and fuses into absorbent surfaces, such as fabric, paper, and wood, to become one with the surface. It will also transfer to nonabsorbent surfaces, but with these it sits *on* the surface rather than fusing into it.

Why Transfer with TAP?

TAP has several advantages over direct printing on fabric:

- Images printed directly on plain fabric are duller and not as sharp as images transferred with TAP. With a printed image, the printer inks are absorbed into the threads of the fabric, which absorb some of the brightness and bleed the sharpness. With a TAP transfer, the polymer coating locks in the brightness and sharpness of the image, so that what you see on the paper is what you get on the fabric.

- When a TAP transfer is done correctly, it is fully washable, even in a bleach cycle. It will retain color and brightness far longer than an image printed directly on plain fabric. Of course, with repeated washings, the TAP transfer will fade over time just as the garment will. But on art quilts, fabric books, ATCs (artist trading cards), or anything else that will not be washed, you can expect long-lasting, colorfast color.

- Transfer TAP onto any fabric without purchasing or preparing your own pretreated fabric. There is no need to trim fabric and back it for your printer. TAP will transfer onto any fabric without any hassles, even after you have pieced or sewn it.

- Draw or create your own artwork with paint, ink, pens, and markers on TAP and transfer it to fabric, resulting in brighter, sharper color than direct-to-fabric applications.

So far, I have only discovered one disadvantage—the polymer that creates all the wonderful benefits listed above will cause some stiffness on the fabric. The stiffness will vary depending on the fabric you use, and it will soften with repeated washings. If the hand of the fabric is more important than the other benefits of TAP, you might prefer direct printing on fabric.

What Can You Transfer with TAP?

When creating with TAP, you can use your own photos, vintage images, or copyright-free images from the Internet that you print from your inkjet printer. You can embellish your printed photos or create stand-alone artwork on TAP. You can transfer any photo, image, drawing, or design that you can print, draw, paint, or stamp onto TAP.

But wait, there's more! (Can you tell how much I love this stuff?) You can combine techniques on one sheet of TAP—print a design, color it in, stamp over it, and then transfer. You can "erase" parts of a photo before transferring by scratching off the polymer coating. You can even iron another transfer or text on top of an already transferred photo. I'll explain how to do all that and more later on in the book.

How TAP Works

TAP is a unique combination of a specialty paper with polymer coating chemically formulated to accept both dye and pigment inkjet printer inks, as well as a number of drawing and painting materials. When heated to approximately 325° (with an iron or heat press), the polymer coating combines with the substances printed or drawn on it, encapsulates them, and fuses into absorbent surfaces, making them permanent, washable, and lightfast. When transferring onto nonabsorbent surfaces, encapsulation occurs, but the transfer sits on the surface and does not fuse into it.

Because TAP was created for fabric transfers, the further away you get from a fabric or fabriclike surface, the more difficulty you will have in getting a perfect transfer. Fabric transfers are always perfect. Glass transfers are the most imperfect. Using TAP on other surfaces is pushing the envelope—something artists do best. Remember, this is a transfer process, and part of the beauty of transferring an image is the imperfections in the end result.

The more you work with TAP, the more experienced you become. Another way of saying *practice makes perfect*.

Care and Handling of TAP

TAP's unique polymer coating requires special care. It is sensitive to moisture and will absorb moisture from the air or will dry out in dry climates. Always store both unprinted and printed TAP in its convenient resealable package or in a similar moisture-proof bag.

The polymer coating is also sensitive to abrasion. It is easily scratched or scraped with sharp objects, even fingernails. Any areas where the coating has been removed, either accidentally or on purpose, will not transfer. Where some may see this as a problem, however, I see possibility. In the section on Beyond the Typical Transfer (pages 25–28), you'll see how this "problem" can work to your advantage.

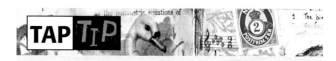

The shelf life of TAP is approximately three years when stored in optimum conditions.

TAP versus Other Transfer Methods

I have been transferring images since 1979 and have earned a reputation as the Transfer Queen in some circles. There are plenty of transfer methods, and I have tried them all, always searching for the "perfect" method. For me, TAP is the perfect method. Once I started TAPping, I never went back. I hope you will feel the same way.

Not all transfer methods are equal. The primary factors for comparison are ease of use, cost, availability, and most important, the end result. Transferring images is both a science and an art. Several variables are always involved:

- The type of paper or surface you transfer from

- The surface you transfer to

- The materials that activate the transfer

- The action that produces the transfer

- The temperature and humidity

- The permanency of the transfer

- The experience of the person doing the transfer

- The desired appearance and degree of perfection of the end result

The benefits of TAP are that it is perhaps the easiest method to use that practically guarantees perfect results, depending on the surface you transfer to. Few, if any, methods can match it for ease, results, and cost effectiveness. I know, because I've tried them all.

TAP Transfer Basics

Printers and Inks

One of the most common questions I get is, "Will TAP work with my printer?" Without even knowing what kind of printer you have, the good news is that the answer is yes, as long as it is an inkjet printer. TAP is not designed for laser (toner-based) printers.

Inkjet printers use two kinds of ink: dye (water-based) ink and pigment inks. For all the transfer methods and direct fabric printing I did in the past, I always preferred and recommended pigment inks for the best results. But that is no longer a consideration, because TAP will work equally well with either type of ink. Your results will be equally vibrant and long-lasting whether your printer uses pigment or dye inks.

Protective Paper and Pressing Cloths

PROTECTIVE PAPER

In the long run, you are going to want to make a habit of using a piece of baking parchment paper or Silicone Release Paper (see Resources, page 63) between your iron and your TAP transfer. When the inks and polymer melt into or onto the receiving surface, be it fabric or any of the other surfaces you can TAP on, the inks can seep beyond the edge of the backing paper and come in contact with your iron. This creates a dirty buildup that can then iron off onto your next project. It's not necessary for the transfer process itself, but using protective paper is a good work habit to follow. I prefer using parchment paper or Silicone Release Paper because you can see through it. That is important so you can see that you are ironing directly onto the TAP.

Using parchment or release paper also enables you to keep your iron moving over the TAP without having the TAP slide around and get off-register or smear. This is particularly helpful when transferring onto surfaces other than fabric, where the TAP is less inclined or unable to fuse into the receiving surface.

Likewise, if you are transferring onto a sheer or semisheer fabric or paper, inks can bleed through to your ironing surface below. A scrap piece of fabric or another sheet of parchment or release paper will keep your ironing board or mat clean as well.

PRESSING CLOTHS

When you are transferring onto less absorbent or non-absorbent surfaces, a pressing cloth or piece of scrap fabric comes in handy. When the polymer has no place to fuse into, it sits on top of the receiving surface rather than fusing completely into the surface. This can happen particularly on glass, but also on wood and some papers. The transfer will feel rough to the touch. That's not a problem, but if you prefer a smooth surface, you can place a piece of fabric over the transfer and iron it again. The excess polymer will then be absorbed into the fabric, resulting in a smooth finish on the original surface.

Use a clean pressing cloth every time so you don't transfer any old excess inks to your new project.

Ironing

IRONS

Ironing instructions call for a hot, dry iron. A hot iron is one set on the highest (usually linen) setting. The steam feature should be turned off. It is recommended that the iron be empty of all water. For the most part, any iron will work, but there are a few things I want to point out about irons.

Many irons have an auto shut-off feature, which will shut off the iron when not used for a time. Always make sure that your iron is hot and has not shut off before beginning a transfer.

If your iron has steam holes, as most newer irons do, you may get a spotted transfer if you don't move the iron gently as you are transferring. This problem can be more apparent on nonabsorbent surfaces. If this becomes a problem, try using the base of the soleplate, which usually has no or fewer steam holes. Another option is to get an older iron, with no steam holes, at a thrift store, yard sale, or Goodwill. You can also purchase one from the Vermont Country Store (see Resources, page 63).

Some travel or craft irons are not designed to be hot enough to produce an optimum TAP transfer. If you are using one of these and not having success, try a standard iron.

Outside the United States, in areas where the voltage is higher, you do not need to have your iron set to the maximum setting. I have found that you can reduce the setting back a bit (cotton or thereabouts) and still get perfect transfers.

IRONING SURFACE

TAP transfers should always be done on a firm, heat-resistant surface. In most cases, your ironing board will work. Some ironing board pads are extra cushioned. If you can make a noticeable indentation with your finger into the pad, then it is probably too thick.

Ironing boards are also rather large, and I'm sure many of you do not always have one set up in your sewing/crafting area. A small, portable ironing board will work, but why not make your own lightweight, portable ironing pad that will work on any available surface? I use a 14" × 22" custom mat that fits both full-sheet and small TAP transfers.

TAPE

When placement counts, tape the TAP in place before ironing. TAP transfers on fabric rarely move, because as soon as the polymer begins to melt from the heat of the iron, the TAP sticks to the fabric. But when even the slightest movement can ruin a project, like on a T-shirt front, give yourself some peace of mind by taping the TAP in place.

Always use a low-tack tape so that the adhesive will not melt into or onto your project and leave any residue. Look for tape advertised as low-tack. I recommend blue painter's tape, which is specifically designed to be low-tack and to not leave residue.

When transferring onto minimally absorbent or nonabsorbent surfaces (wood, metal, mica, glass), taping TAP in place will ensure that is does not slip, slide, or smear.

Bonus Ironing Mat

materials

14" × 22" piece of heat-resistant fabric designed for potholders

14" × 22" piece of Insul-Fleece or Warm & Natural batting

20" × 28" piece of cotton fabric

Pins

Iron

Sewing machine

construction

1. Fold under the edges of the cotton fabric ½" to enclose the raw edges. Iron in place.

2. Place the fabric right side down, and center the batting or Insul-Fleece on the fabric leaving a 3" margin on each side.

3. Place the heat-resistant fabric, shiny side up, on top of the batting.

4. Fold the fabric toward the front over both the batting and heat-resistant fabric.

5. Miter the corners as if wrapping a package, and iron in place.

6. Pin the fabric to secure the layers. Use a straight or zigzag stitch to sew down the edge of the fabric where it meets the heat-resistant fabric.

Prepare Your Photos for Fabulous Transfers

You will always get great results when you transfer your photos with TAP. You will always get fabulous results when you start with a great photo. I'm not talking about your oh-so-cute new puppy, darling granddaughter, or that awesome island sunset (although I'm sure they are great photos). I'm talking about preparing your photo for maximum impact and appearance. I'm talking about cropping, contrast, brightness, and saturation.

To optimize your photos you need a photo-editing software program. You very likely already have one on your computer. The type of adjustments you need to make to your photos for optimal results can be done with any level of photo-editing software, from the ones that come with your computer (iPhoto and Windows Photo Gallery); to free ones, such as Google's Picasa; to the top-of-the-line, multifunction programs like Adobe Photoshop, Photoshop Elements, and Corel Paint Shop Pro.

The how-tos of editing photos could take up this whole book. Many excellent books and online tutorials are available (see Resources, page 63) if you wish to go beyond the basic instructions below. I must warn you, once you start, you may fall down the rabbit hole of photo-editing. It's fun and addictive.

Materials and Equipment

Photograph

Scanner or all-in-one printer

Computer

Photo-editing software

Printer

TAP

Six Steps to Success

1. Scan photo(s) into your computer

Set the scanner for 300 ppi (pixels per inch) or 300 resolution. A high resolution enables you to enlarge the photo and still have a high-quality print. If you have a very small photo, such as 2″ or smaller on any side, and you want to print it larger than 5″ on any side, scan it at 600 ppi/resolution so that you can enlarge it to your desired size and get a good print.

After resizing (page 10), save the photo at 300 ppi/resolution for optimum print quality. Any more than that is unnecessary and will not improve the quality of your printed photo.

Original scanned photo

Scratches removed

Cropped photo

Auto Contrast applied

2. Erase Flaws or Spots

There are several ways to correct scratches, age spots, or spots. I use the *Healing Brush* tool (Band-Aid icon) or the *Smudge* tool in Photoshop or Photoshop Elements. Refer to your photo-editing software for ways to erase or fill in flaws.

3. Resize and Crop

If you want to change the size of the photo, now is the time. Refer to your photo-editing program for instructions on resizing images.

Many old photos will look better in your finished art if you zoom in on the subject and crop out the rest of the background. A tighter shot creates better impact. Play around with the *Crop* tool in your photo-editing software, and crop the photo so it looks best to you and works for your project. After cropping, resize the photo again so it is the finished size you want to use in your artwork.

4. Enhance Contrast

Age does a number on photos. Almost all black-and-white photos fade to neutral grays. Color photos fade to pastels. Adjusting the *contrast* in your photo-editing software will bring some life back into the photo. I almost always use the *Auto Contrast* function. Refer to your photo-editing software for instructions on improving contrast.

TAP TIP

It is smart at this time, if you have not already done so, to create a new, separate folder on your computer for the photos you have enhanced. You can also create a folder inside the new photo folder for each project or category of photo, such as family, holiday, nature, and so on.

Auto Color applied

Auto Levels applied

5. Correct Color

If your photo has yellowed, you may want to remove some or all of the yellowing. I will often leave a bit so that the photo still has somewhat of an aged look to it. The method to use depends on the functions available in your photo-editing software. Many programs have auto functions for color correction. *Auto Levels* will often correct the color to its original appearance. If you are not confident in your skills, the auto functions are the way to go.

6. Increase Saturation

Saturation refers to the intensity of the color in the photo. I always used to bump up the color saturation of all my photos when I was printing directly onto fabric. Direct fabric printing, even on pretreated fabric, dulls the color a bit because the printer inks are absorbed into the fabric. This does not happen when you do a TAP transfer. The inks are encapsulated into the polymer coating on the paper and remain bright and saturated. But, I still like to bump up the saturation of my photos for greater impact. A camera can only capture so much, and a photo is always affected by lighting. If you feel your photo is lacking in color, increase the color saturation. Refer to your photo-editing software for specific directions.

Original photo

Increased saturation to pop color

Adjust and Enhance Black-and-White Photos

Black-and-white photos need a little different treatment to be at their best. The following is a visual example of what to do.

Original photo

Healing Brush tool used to erase scratches and fold marks

Auto Contrast applied

Cropped and brightness increased

Auto Levels applied

Prepare a Photo for Printing

A transfer is a mirror-image process. In other words, the completed transfer is backward, or the reverse of the original. To transfer a photo, you must print it in reverse so that the finished transfer looks like the original. In some instances it won't matter if it is reversed, and you can choose to use it either way. If your photo is of someone you know or there is any text, you absolutely need to print in reverse. Our faces are not 100% symmetrical, so if you print your own photo or a photo of someone you know without reversing it first, the person in the transferred image will look quite strange to you. Likewise, text will be backward and unreadable.

You can reverse your photos in photo-editing software or when you go to the *Print* function for your printer. On the *Print* screen, find the *Properties* tab. Depending on the printer or photo-editing program terminology, choose either *Rotate/Flip Horizontal, Mirror Image, Transfer Printing, Invert Image,* or *T-Shirt Transfer.*

The Transfer Process

I have been transferring and teaching transfers for more than ten years. No matter what your primary medium is—fabric, paper, metal, wood, glass, or polymer clay—I always recommend learning a transfer process on fabric. This is because fabric is both absorbent and forgiving. Absorbent means that fabric will easily absorb the transfer medium. Forgiving means that should you under- or overwork the transfer process, the fabric will not tear, flake, puddle, or peel away when you remove the transfer paper. Most of these concerns are not applicable for TAP transfers, but I still recommend that you start with fabric.

TAP was designed for transfers onto fabric. That is where it will perform the best. If you are a beginner, the further you get away from fabric, the more unpredictable your results will be. Until you get familiar with the process, start easy.

After a few fabric transfers, try paper, lots of different papers. Next, move on to wood, then metal. Each move to a less absorbent surface will create less-than-perfect and unpredictable results. It is important to test and get a feel for how TAP works on different surfaces before diving right into your project. Transferring images is both an art and a science, and as with any skill, practice leads to success.

Basic TAP Transfer Instructions

These basic instructions for TAP transfers are specifically for transferring onto fabrics, but they apply to all surfaces except as noted in the following sections, which include additional specific directions for transferring onto less absorbent and nonabsorbent surfaces.

1. Print or draw the selected image(s) in reverse onto the white side of a sheet of TAP (page 12).

2. Preheat the iron to the highest setting. *Do not use steam.*

3. Trim any excess paper from around the image if desired.

4. Place the fabric right side up on a firm ironing surface.

5. Place the TAP, image side down, onto fabric, and cover with parchment or release paper (page 7).

6. Iron the TAP with a continuous motion, making sure to cover the entire surface.

7. Iron for at least 30–90 seconds or until the TAP lifts easily from the fabric.

Ironing time will depend on the size of the transfer and its intended final use. To ensure washability, iron until the transfer is 100% complete. When it is completed, the image side of TAP should feel smooth to the touch, with no remaining polymer. If your transfer image will not be washed, it's okay to use a shorter ironing time, as long as your image is transferred to your satisfaction.

TAP is a hot-peel transfer paper, meaning that you must peel away the paper from the completed transfer while it is still hot. Do not let it cool in place. It's okay to rewarm a stubborn edge, but never let the paper cool completely, because it can result in the transfer sticking to the paper, creating an incomplete image.

It's easy to check the status of your transfer by peeling back a corner to check, and then continue to iron over it if the transfer is not complete.

The how-tos and the pros and cons of TAP transfers as they pertain to the most common art and craft surfaces are discussed in this chapter. If you have one in mind that you do not see here, try it! If you can iron it, it just might work. And then be sure and share your discovery with us online at http://www.flickr.com/groups/happytappers/.

This tip applies to any and all surfaces and all transfer methods. All transfers, including TAP transfers, work best when you are transferring to a smooth surface. If the surface you are transferring to has a high point, such as a fabric slub, a thick brush stroke, or a rough and uneven wood surface, then when you iron or burnish the image onto that uneven surface, the ink will transfer to the high point, leaving a halo area around the high point where no ink transfers. Depending on the overall look you want, that's not always a problem, but do keep it in mind when you choose a surface to transfer onto.

TAP on fabric

Stitched TAP

Julie's Dream by Theresa Martin

You can apply TAP to 100% cotton, blends, silk, sheers, polyester, spandex, Lycra, genuine leather, vintage fabrics, and more. If you want to use a fabric that cannot take the high heat TAP requires, use parchment or release paper or a pressing cloth between the iron and the TAP paper to protect the fabric underneath. For cottons, TAP works best on a medium thread count fabric (60 × 60 threads/per inch, such as Kona cotton); using a higher thread count often makes the fabric too stiff.

Fabric or garment prewashing is not necessary unless you want to preshrink it in preparation for future washings.

TAP on leather

1

2

3

TAP on white and dark backgrounds

TAP on printed fabric with die-cut letter
cut out and removed from image before transfer

TAP on vintage damask

TAP on felt

TAP on lamé

Layered TAP on sheer over muslin

Left: TAP on muslin; Right: TAP on sheer

PROS

■ TAP was made for fabric. Once transferred, the image is fused into the fibers of the fabric and becomes one with the fabric. It becomes a part of the material with a smooth, almost silky, feel (depending on the fabric). There is no edge to the transfer, so it will not lift or peel off.

■ You can stitch through TAP transfers without harming your machine or the image.

■ TAP has been designed to produce bright, sharp, permanent images on fabric, even after washing and even when using bleach.

■ TAP is great for T-shirts because you can stretch it and it will not crack. After the image has cooled, you can stretch the fabric and it will have no impact on the image. TAP on t-shirt knits is soft and pliable and not stiff like on other fabrics.

■ You can iron directly over a TAP transfer. This means you can iron another TAP transfer (or three or four) right on top of an already transferred image.

■ TAP will transfer onto a sheer or open-weave fabric. Because of the open weave, some of the ink will also transfer to the ironing surface below. Why is this a good thing? I call it a two-fer: Place a piece of fabric (or paper) underneath the sheer, and the excess ink will transfer onto that surface, resulting in a second transferred image that you can use in other art. Or you could keep it under the original sheer transfer to add a beautiful layer of depth to the original image.

Turn garments inside out before washing to protect your transfer from abrasion. I'm not saying it will look like new forever—no fabric ever does after repeated washing—but with proper care, a TAP transfer will fare far better than all other transferred or screened images.

Acrylic paint applied to photo after transfer to show areas of untrimmed polymer.

Photo trimmed before transfer.

Large, untrimmed border.

Untrimmed images cause uneven absorption of paint if applied after transfer.

CONS

■ The clear polymer coating on TAP paper will always transfer as clear but can be noticeable on dark fabrics. Avoid this by trimming (or scratching, page 25) any excess white areas when possible.

■ The polymer that produces such bright, sharp, durable images also leaves a residue on the fabric, making the image area stiffer. How stiff will depend on the type of fabric you use. Most TAP users consider this a small price to pay for the end result.

■ TAP transfers (like all transfers) are transparent, so your color images will look best on white or light-colored fabrics. Use a strong-contrast or black-and-white image on darker fabrics.

TAP on various papers

TAP on vintage dictionary page

TAP on scrapbook paper

TAP on paper

Next to fabric, paper is the most popular surface for TAP transfers. TAP will readily fuse into all uncoated papers. TAP is an excellent way to get images onto papers that you cannot put through your printer.

PROS

■ TAP can be transferred on papers that are too delicate, thick, or large to fit into your inkjet printer.

■ TAP works beautifully on delicate Japanese papers that don't have enough body to go through your printer.

■ You can do a TAP transfer onto a surface you are already working on—something you wouldn't or couldn't put into your printer.

■ You can transfer directly into a journal, altered book, or scrapbook.

■ Create custom cards, artist trading cards, or calling cards.

CONS

■ TAP transfers (like all transfers) are transparent, so your color images will look best on white or light-colored papers. Use a strong-contrast or black-and-white image on darker papers.

■ TAP transfers best onto smooth papers, so you may not be happy with your results when using some of the art papers that have a rough texture, such as rough watercolor paper or abaca paper.

■ When transferring onto glossy or coated papers, the transfer will sit *on* the paper and feel rough to the touch. For a smoother feel, place a piece of fabric on the transfer and iron over it. The fabric will absorb the excess and smooth out the transfer (page 7).

TAP on stretched canvas

If you are a painter or use stretched canvas or canvas boards as a base for your artwork, you will be happy to know that you can TAP on your canvasses. Read the Pros and Cons below to ensure your success.

PROS

■ Transfer an image onto your canvas to use as a guide for your painting—a sophisticated "paint-by-number" approach.

■ Transfer onto a blank or color-washed canvas and paint around it for a combination of realism and painting.

■ Add a transferred image to a work in progress.

■ Incorporate text and flourishes into your work that would be hard to reproduce by hand.

CONS

■ When using a stretched canvas, you need to put a support behind the canvas so it is firm enough to create a good transfer. A stack of index cards fits nicely inside the back of a 5″ × 7″ stretched canvas. Books work well behind 8″ × 10″ and larger canvasses. You only need to support the area where you are transferring.

■ Ironing over the stretcher bars is tricky because they are not always flat. There may be some imperfectly transferred areas where you are not ironing over perfectly flat, smooth surfaces.

■ If you transfer over thicker applications of paint, the paint will bubble as a result of the heat of the iron, and your transfer will have a distressed appearance.

■ Any roughness due to brushstrokes or layered surfaces on the canvas will interfere with a perfect transfer, since all transfers work best on smooth surfaces. If perfection is your goal, transfer onto fabric or paper, and then add it to your canvas.

TAP on Lutradur laced by heat gun after transfer

Ultra-Light Lutradur creates pattern on TAP-transferred image.

TAP on lutradur

I think of Lutradur as the magic in the middle—a sturdy art surface with the best attributes of both fabric and paper. It is created from spun polymer fibers pressed into sheets. If you are not familiar with Lutradur, I encourage you to explore the possibilities with my book *Fabulous Fabric Art with Lutradur*, also available from C&T.

Lutradur and TAP appear to be made for each other. Not only do TAP transfers on Lutradur feel smooth and silky, but also the transparent nature and firm body of the (70gm and 100gm) Lutradur enable you to create exciting three-dimensional artwork, books, and more.

TAP transfer on painted Lutradur; Lutradur design created with Walnut Hollow Creative Textile Tool

TAP layered over Angelina film and fibers, then ironed

PROS

■ TAP transfers can be done on white or painted Lutradur. Any background color will affect the colors in the transferred image; for examples, see *Solitude vs. Lonely* (page 38).

■ Transfer onto white Lutradur; then paint Lutradur. You can paint over and TAP transfer.

■ A TAP transfer will act as a resist for any heat techniques you use on Lutradur.

■ TAP transfers on Lutradur can be sewn, glued, fused, and so forth. In other words, treat Lutradur like any fabric or paper.

CONS

■ Because both TAP and Lutradur are made with polymer (plastic), they tend to fuse together from the heat of the iron and the TAP paper will not easily lift away when the transfer is complete. Once you see that the transfer is complete, gently peel it away while still hot.

■ Lutradur is transparent, so always place parchment or release paper or scrap fabric under the Lutradur before ironing to catch any inks that seep through.

TAP TIP

Use Ultra-Light (25gm) Lutradur to create a crackled or spider web pattern on your image: Choose a base fabric, layer 25gm Lutradur over the fabric, transfer the image, and voilá!

TAP on wood

Unfinished wood is another absorbent surface that is relatively easy to transfer onto. I've tried several unfinished wood surfaces and have found that they can vary by quality, which therefore affects the quality of the TAP transfer. A wood surface can look smooth but is often very grainy, especially in the more inexpensive unfinished wood products. I recommend the top-quality unfinished wood products from Walnut Hollow (see Resources, page 63) for the best results.

TAP transfers work best on unfinished, stained, or color-washed wood. Painting or varnishing will seal the wood, and the transfer will sit on top of the wood rather than be fused into it.

Paper towels will work in place of fabric to smooth out rough transfers on nonabsorbent surfaces, but if the towels are embossed, they may leave signs of the pattern on the transfer. It may be a problem, or it may be a bonus design element … you decide.

PROS

■ TAP transfers become an integral part of the wood and can be sealed after the transfer to give them a gloss, shine, or just protection.

■ You can color wash the wood with acrylic inks or watered-down acrylic paints (see Resources, page 63) for a tinted background color before transferring.

■ Try doing a wash of color over the completed transfer.

■ Paint, stain, or decorate any remaining exposed wood after completing the transfer. Use low-tack painter's masking tape to protect the transfer if necessary.

CONS

■ Transferring onto painted wood is difficult but not impossible. When you heat wood painted with acrylic paint, it will react with the heat and may melt, bubble, or crack depending on the thickness of the paint. Test by painting some wood scraps, let the paint dry at least 48 hours, and practice some transfers. You might like the results, depending on the look you are going for.

■ What looks and feels like smooth wood isn't always smooth. Depending on the quality of the wood, the grain is tighter on some woods than others. Just as a tighter weave of fabric results in a sharply detailed transfer, a tight, smooth woodgrain is best for "perfect" transfers. If possible, get extra wood so that you can test the wood to see how it absorbs the transfer. You can do some light sanding if necessary or do a thin wash of fluid acrylic medium to give a light seal to the grain, followed by a light sanding to create a smoother base for the transfer.

■ Transfers will not work on rounded, concave, or carved wood surfaces because these are difficult to impossible to iron evenly.

TAP on Walnut Hollow brass craft metal

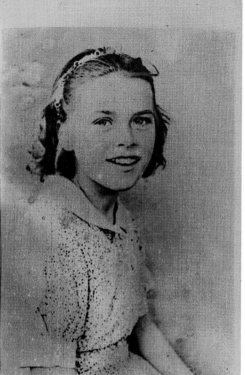

TAP on heat-patinaed copper mesh

TAP on vintage glass bottle

TAP on mica

TAP on metal duct tape from hardware store

Additional Directions for Nonabsorbent Surfaces (Metal, Mica, Glass, Polymer Clay)

Transferring onto nonabsorbent surfaces is not as straightforward as transferring onto fabric and paper. Before beginning, be sure to read the following directions as well as the specific notes for each surface.

1. Tape TAP in place before ironing, and use parchment or release paper between the TAP and the iron.

2. Avoid sliding the iron too much; instead, use more of a press-and-lift motion.

3. The transfer usually occurs in **seconds**. Avoid overironing, which will smear the image.

4. The transfer will feel rough. If you prefer a smooth finish, place a piece of fabric on top of the transfer, and then iron. The fabric will absorb and smooth out the excess polymer.

on Walnut Hollow copper square stitched onto painted watercolor paper, ribbon embellishment

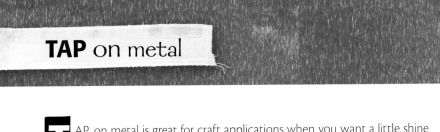

TAP on metal

PROS

■ Emboss the metal after transferring to add texture and dimension to the image.

■ Easily scratch away any unwanted areas before the polymer cures (usually 48–96 hours).

CONS

■ White areas in the image will appear as cloudy white areas in the finished transfer because of the metallic shine of the metal. Trim away as much white as possible from the TAP before transferring.

■ Images can flake or scratch off if subject to rough abrasion; treat the transferred work as you would any art.

■ Some metals may have a film of oil on them that will interfere with the transfer. If it feels oily or greasy, clean with isopropyl alcohol.

■ Thicker metals may take longer to heat up with the iron and will remain hotter longer.

TAP on metal is great for craft applications when you want a little shine in a project, but metal is a tricky, nonabsorbent surface. Most important, metal gets *hot* when ironed. It is important to peel the paper while it's still hot, so I use a bit of folded fabric to hold down the hot metal while I slide the tip of my X-ACTO knife under the edge. Once the paper begins to lift, finish peeling with your finger.

TAP transfers on metal are best when done on thin metal sheets or metal mesh from craft stores or Walnut Hollow (Resources, page 63). Transfers occur in seconds, and overironing will create a goopy mess of the image due to the intense heat. Transfers look best on lighter metals, such as aluminum and copper, but can be done on any color. Just remember that the colors of the image will change (or even disappear), depending on the color of the metal.

TAP transfers onto metal only take about 5 to 10 seconds. It is important to iron evenly over the entire piece in that time. Do not overiron. Overironing causes the inks to stick back on the TAP paper backing and will result in a splotchy transfer.

TAP on mica

Mica is a natural silicate mineral. It is transparent and can vary in color from clear to smoky to amber, depending on the mine it comes from. TAP transfers on mica can resemble glass and are great for layering or using when you need a bit of transparency in a project.

When working with mica, tape the printed TAP in place. The transfer will occur quickly, within seconds; then peel the paper while hot.

PROS

■ You can transfer to either side of mica.

■ If you transfer on the back or reverse side of the mica, you do not need to reverse the image before printing.

■ TAP on mica is a great way to add another dimension to your art to create windows, layers, and so on.

CONS

■ White areas in the image will appear as cloudy white areas in the finished transfer because of the transparency of the mica. Trim away as much white as possible before transferring.

■ Images can flake or scratch off if subject to rough abrasion; treat them as you would any art.

TAP on glass

TAP transfers are transparent. Glass is transparent. It wasn't much of a leap for me to TAP on glass. It is also the trickiest surface to work on because glass is non-absorbent, retains heat, and has the potential of cracking when heated rapidly. It is one of the trickiest surfaces to master, and even then results are not guaranteed. Use the following additional directions to ensure safety and success.

1. Position and tape TAP (image side down) on glass with low-tack tape, and cover with parchment or release paper.

2. Start with a cool iron. Turn the dial to the highest setting, and place on the TAP and glass.

3. Keep the iron moving while it heats up. After the TAP reaches the correct temperature to activate the transfer, you are done. Do not overiron. If you iron too long, the inks/polymer will smear.

4. The glass will be hot. Use pliers or tweezers to peel back a corner of the paper to check the completeness of the transfer. If you are satisfied, remove the paper and let the glass cool. Always peel hot; do not let the TAP cool on the glass.

5. If the finished transfer feels rough and you want it smooth, place a piece of fabric on top of the transfer and iron (starting with cool iron as in Step 2). The fabric will absorb and smooth out the excess polymer.

PROS

■ You can transfer on either side of the glass.

■ If you transfer on the back or reverse side of the glass, you do not need to reverse the image before printing.

■ TAP on glass is a great way to add another dimension to framed artwork.

CONS

■ White areas in the image will appear as cloudy white areas in the finished transfer because of the transparency of the glass. Trim away as much white as possible before transferring.

■ You can only transfer onto smooth, flat glass surfaces.

■ Dark colors transfer best. Pale or pastel colors don't show up as well.

■ Images can flake or scratch off if subject to rough abrasion; treat them as you would any art.

TAP TIP

Glass cracks when it gets too hot, so always start with a cool iron and heat the glass and TAP paper at the same time. Do not use tempered glass. It is heat-resistant.

TAP on vintage glass bottle

TAP on polymer clay

Polymer clay and TAP are both made with polymers. There are several ways to transfer onto polymer clay, and the advantage of using TAP is that when you marry one polymer with another, it becomes permanent. After several experiments, polymer clay expert Martina Webb came up with this set of instructions for optimum TAP transfer on polymer.

1. Print in reverse (page 12) or otherwise apply decoration to transfer onto TAP. Cut out the imagery with a ⅛" margin.

2. Roll out the polymer clay slightly larger than the final piece.

3. Apply a very thin layer of liquid polymer clay (Liquid Sculpey) to create a slightly tacky surface.

4. Apply TAP, image side down. Lightly rub the back of the TAP with a finger to adhere the TAP to the clay.

5. Apply water one drop at a time to the back of the TAP until the paper has absorbed the water and you can see the image through the backing. Let this sit for 30 minutes.

6. Rewet the surface until barely damp. Thoroughly burnish the entire surface in all directions with the back of a spoon using moderate pressure.

7. Starting at a corner, slowly peel away the TAP backing paper. If you see any untransferred areas, lay the TAP back down and reburnish that area. Remove all the paper.

8. Tiny flecks of missing color can be repaired by using a pin to remove any flecks still adhering to the TAP and gently filling in the hole on your work. You can also repair a piece after baking using acrylic paint or a Sharpie marker in a matching color.

9. Cut out the polymer clay piece using a downward chopping motion, not a slicing sideways motion. Avoid distorting the surface of the transfer as it can crack at this stage.

10. Bake per the manufacturer's instructions. Allow the piece to cool completely before removing it from the oven.

11. To flatten any bubbles that may occur, cover the piece with parchment or Silicone Release Paper. Press with an iron on the lowest setting for 5–10 seconds without moving the iron.

12. For pendants, insert the findings before baking. Make U-shaped wires or purchase silver-plated screw eyes. Mark the spot with the end of the finding, make a fine hole using a sharp needle, and then insert the finding using pliers. Try not to make the hole any larger than the diameter of the finding. After baking, remove the finding to do any sanding and smoothing. Glue the findings in place.

PROS

■ Transfers are made on unbaked clay so you can trim around your image before baking.

■ TAP polymer is baked onto polymer clay, so it is scratch resistant.

■ Printing, drawing, or coloring small images for polymer transfers is a great way to fill up any extra space on a sheet of TAP when printing larger images for transfer.

CONS

■ TAP transfers on polymer require an additional accelerant or activator.

■ It's the most complicated TAP transfer process, requiring several steps and additional time.

■ Results are not instant as with the other TAP transfers.

Angel photo transferred onto tree-landscaped transfer.

Central trees scratched away to make room for angel layer.

Stars and moon scratched into printed image before transfer

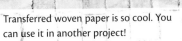

Transferred woven paper is so cool. You can use it in another project!

In another example, areas of some TAP images were masked from transferring to surface by another piece of TAP.

TAP transferred onto brown paper bag painted with gold metallic paint prior to transfer.

Scratch

Scratching TAP removes the polymer coating that both creates the transfer and locks the inks into the transferred surface. This technique can be used to create decorative white areas or a distressed grunge look on your images. It is also a way to remove unwanted areas from the image instead of trimming with scissors or a craft knife such as an X-ACTO knife.

Be practical or get creative. I have used my fingernail, an X-ACTO knife, and similar sharp tools to "erase" areas or draw into the polymer. I particularly like to scratch into the edges of an image to give it a less-than-perfect look.

Layer and Mask

One of the wonderful features of TAP is that you are able to iron right over a completed transfer. This is great for garments and quilts in progress, which need a lot of ironing. But you can also use this feature as an art technique.

Build up layers of transfer by transferring one image on top of another one or two or three images. Yes, you can layer in photo-editing software, but sometimes (always?) creating doesn't happen in a linear process, and you might find yourself saying, "I wish I had placed that word on the image before I printed it." Well you can do that just by ironing another transfer right on top of the first one.

Remember that transfers are transparent, so if there is a part of an image that will interfere with the next layer, just scratch it away (page 25) **before** transferring.

Another way to use layers is to print several photos on TAP and create a montage, overlapping trimmed photos into a pleasing arrangement. You have to do a little planning ahead and work in reverse.

1. Trim all the images to size.

2. Arrange them right on your ironing surface so you don't have to move anything.

3. Place the fabric or paper on *top* of the montage and iron away.

Starting with blank paper, TAP paper was taped back in place after transfer to create a mask over the image while paint and pattern were applied.

Remember that the final montage will be a reverse of the one you created, so keep that in mind as you are designing.

When you layer one image on top of another, you are creating a mask, because the TAP paper will mask or block the image area on the photo underneath. What will happen is that this masked area will transfer onto the TAP paper on top of it, not onto your fabric or other surface. Imagine the possibilities!

Weave

One of my favorite techniques is to weave left-over strips of printed TAP and transfer them to fabric to create a one-of-a-kind fabric to use in other projects. An open weave allows the color of the paper or fabric to show through.

In addition to using leftovers, you can choose two or more photos and print each of them on the full 8½″ × 11″ sheet of TAP. I like to tear the strips for a more organic look, but you can cut them to get a tighter weave. Chose photos with similar colors or create contrast by using opposites. I take a lot of texture and pattern photos, which really work well for the weaving technique.

Woven TAP strips transferred onto very absorbent printmaking paper create a stunning work of art.

Mosaic

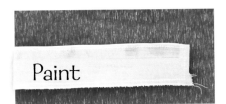

Here's another fun and easy TAP technique. Create mosaics by cutting a photo into pieces. Kids love this. Create fractured portraits, leaving room for a quote or poem, or add another photo in between. In other words, play!

Mosaic portrait

Paint

Here's a surprising fact: I've already told you that TAP must be stored in a plastic bag because it is sensitive to moisture and should not get wet. Don't ask me how this works, because even the chemists are surprised, but you can paint on TAP. Yes, you can use watercolors, water-soluble crayons, watered down acrylics, and inks.

I believe the secret is in transferring the painted paper immediately after it air dries, usually within 10–20 minutes. I have put it in front of a fan or under a lamp to speed it up but would not suggest using a heat gun, which may begin to melt the polymer coating.

Image drawn on TAP with Pigma Micron marker, then painted prior to transfer with watered-down Liquitex Soft Body Acrylics

Judy Coates Perez's project *A Matter of Perspective* (page 48) was created with watercolor crayons blended with a wet paintbrush. If she had followed the rules about not getting TAP wet, her beautiful quilt would have never happened. Lesson? Art happens when you try breaking the rules!

Completed transfer—image is reverse of original drawing.

Another way to use paint on TAP is after the transfer.

Use a TAP image as a base and guide for painting on fabric, paper, canvas, leather, wood, and more.

Color

TAP paper first wiped with gold PearlEx powder; then thistle image stamped onto TAP.

ere's where TAP gets fun! You don't have to just print photos on it. You can draw, color, stamp, paint, add chalks, powders, and more. Not sure if something will work? Experiment! The only caveat is that you don't want to use anything that will scratch off the polymer coating. No coating, no transfer.

You would think a ball-point pen would scratch the surface, but not when used with a light hand in the piece by Nina Perez (bottom right).

In the following sample, a black-and-white image was colored prior to transfer using the following materials: dress colored with Staedtler Karat Aquarell crayons; waistband colored with Pigma Micron pen; background colored with chalk ink stamp pad; rug colored with marker; and armrest colored with soft body acrylic paint.

Left: Colored TAP paper
Right: Completed transfer

The polymer on TAP seals the surface of the fabric, so you can get a nice sharp painted line that won't bleed.

Addition of paint enhances this TAP transfer, which has been mounted on fast2fuse. Excess fabric was folded and fused to back of piece. Edge of image was defined with acrylic ink.

Testing 1-2-3: Test page of black-and-white images colored with variety of art materials prior to transferring, by Liz Kettle

Floral Anatomy by Nina Perez

Image drawn on TAP before transfer onto raw canvas using ball-point pen; red halo painted with CretaColor AquaStic; yellow flowers colored after transfer with Copic Marker

projects

Quote Box

If we follow the individual
wisdom and uniqueness
in each of us, we will
find expression and creativity
beyond our wildest dreams.

Lane Arye

By Lesley Riley

This box is the perfect size for index cards. I use it to store some of my favorite quotes.

Materials

Small Ball Foot Lancaster Trunk
by Walnut Hollow

Quotes printed in reverse on TAP
(page 12)

Parchment paper or Silicone Release
Paper (Resources, page 63)

Liquitex Ink (Cerulean Blue)

Liquitex Soft Body Acrylic
(Cadmium Red Light)

Liquitex Matte Gel Medium

Wood doll head/knob 1½″
(from craft store)

Screw and washer to fit knob

Drill

Instructions

See basic transfer instructions (page 13) and TAP on Wood (page 19).

1. Measure the sides and top of the box to determine the size of the text blocks.

2. Use word processing to type each quote to a specific size. Choose a font that best fits the dimensions. Test print on plain paper to confirm the size and placement, and adjust the font size if necessary.

3. Lightly sand the box, and then wipe it with a moist paper towel to remove sanding dust.

4. Stain the box with a watered-down wash of acrylic ink. Sand lightly, and wipe off the dust again when dry.

5. Cut the printed TAP to size. Working with one quote at a time, tape each quote facedown in place, and iron to transfer.

6. After transferring all of the quotes, seal the box and transfers with a coat of acrylic medium.

7. Paint the knob. When it is dry, seal it with acrylic medium.

8. Drill a hole in the center of the box lid for the knob screw.

9. Screw the knob to the box lid.

Jillian

Jillian
November 16, 2009

By Lesley Riley

I have had the honor of being present at the birth of three of my granddaughters, not only as the grandma but also as the official photographer. I loved chronicling the hours leading up to Jillian's birth and the subsequent shots of her as she grew. The best part ... she was born on my birthday!

Materials

1 sheet 22″ × 30″ of hot press (smooth) watercolor paper (creates 9 pages 10″ × 7″)

Images and text (sized to fill a 5″ × 7″ page) printed in reverse on TAP (page 12)

Parchment paper or Silicone Release Paper (Resources, page 63)

Acrylic paints or inks

Foam brushes

12″ ruler

Instructions

See basic transfer instructions (page 13) and TAP on Paper (page 16).

1. Paint the watercolor paper in pale washes of color that will be the backgrounds for your photo transfers. Make sure the washes are light enough so that the background colors won't interfere with the coloring or subject matter in the photos you will be transferring.

2. Measure and cut or tear the paper into several 10″ × 7″ pieces. Fold each sheet in half to 5″ × 7″ size.

3. Determine the placement of your photos, and using the fold line as a guide, transfer each image to a page. Option: If you have a suitable photo, print it at 10″ × 7″ size and transfer along the length of the centermost page spread— the one that opens to show both sides of the same sheet at the same time. Another idea is to print a large word, poem, or message to fill the 10″ × 7″ page.

4. Add any additional text transfers as desired on top of the transferred photos.

5. When all the transfers are complete, add additional embellishment to the pages as desired.

6. Binding is optional; use your preferred method.

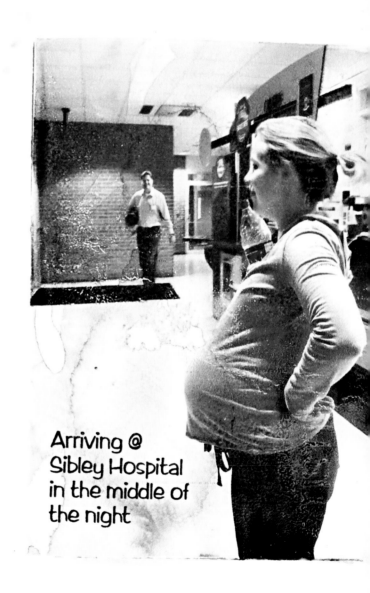

Arriving @ Sibley Hospital in the middle of the night

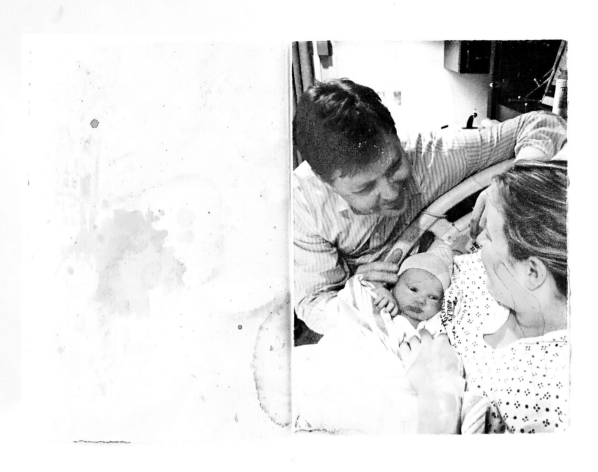

Lines:
A Zipper Quilt

By Lesley Riley

One use of TAP is to create your own custom TAP fabric. In this quilt, I used five pattern photos taken at a shipyard to create 8½″ × 11″ pieces of fabric that I turned into a quilt. I used gold metal coat zippers to give the quilt more of a hard-edged feeling and to accent the many lines in the fabric.

Materials

White fabric cut into 8½" × 11" pieces, 1 piece for each photo

8" × 10½" photos printed in reverse on TAP (page 12)

Parchment paper or Silicone Release Paper (Resources, page 63)

Sewing machine and sewing thread

Batting

Backing fabric

Zippers (optional); I used 4 zippers 12" long.

PearlEx Powders and acrylic spray finish (optional)

Instructions

See basic transfer instructions (page 13) and TAP on Fabric (pages 14–15).

1. Transfer the printed images to fabric, placing the images so that there is a ¼" white margin on the fabric that will serve as your sewing lines and seam allowances.

2. Arrange and stitch the printed photos (right sides together) to form the quilt top.

3. Decide on the placement of the zippers (if you are using them), and pin them in place. Stitch the zippers to the quilt top—use a zipper foot or open the zipper to move the pull tab as it gets close to the presser foot.

4. Cut the batting to the size of the quilt top.

5. Cut the backing fabric to the size of the finished quilt plus ¼" seam allowance on all sides.

6. Place the quilt backing and the quilt top right sides together, and pin around all 4 sides. Place the batting on top, centering it inside of the quilt top seam allowances (the photo edges).

7. Sew around all 4 edges, leaving an opening large enough to turn the quilt inside out.

8. Trim the corners at a 45° angle, and turn the quilt inside out. Press, and stitch the opening closed.

9. Machine or hand quilt as desired.

10. Embellish as desired. I highlighted areas of the quilt with PearlEx powders to give it some iridescence and shimmer, and then sealed the powders with a light acrylic spray finish.

Solitude vs. Lonely

By Lesley Riley

Materials

Lutradur for your desired page size and number of pages

Images and favorite quotes or other text printed in reverse on TAP (page 12)

Parchment paper or Silicone Release Paper (Resources, page 63)

Liquitex Soft Body Acrylic Paints and/or Inks and brushes

Fabric scraps

A sturdy ribbon at least 1½″ wide and the length of the book height for binding

Wonder-Under fusible web

Sewing machine and sewing thread

For the blackest blacks, select Black Ink Only on your printer menu, usually found in the Advanced menu.

Instructions

See basic transfer instructions (page 13) and TAP on Lutradur (page 63).

1. Lutradur is translucent, so each transferred photo will be visible on both the front and back of each page. Count the photos you want to use to determine your page count, which should always be an even number (9 photos = 10 pages). You do not need a photo on the back cover, and each page will only need one photo since the pages are translucent.

2. Paint the Lutradur in soft colors with watered-down acrylic paints or inks, and allow them to dry thoroughly. Cut the Lutradur into spreads. A spread is twice as wide as your desired finished page width and the same height as the desired finished page. Five spreads will create a 10-page book. Fold each spread in half to create 2 pages.

3. Determine which photos you want on each page, and transfer them to the painted Lutradur.

4. Choose fabric that coordinates with each photo, and transfer the quote for that photo to that fabric. Machine or hand stitch in place on the page. Add additional stitching, embellishment, or decoration as desired.

5. Cut the binding ribbon to size, and iron paper-backed fusible web to the wrong side. Leave the paper on, and fold the ribbon in half lengthwise. Iron to set the fold, and then remove the paper.

6. Stack the pages together in the correct order, and fold so that the cover is on top. Clamp around the open edges with clamps or clothespins to prevent shifting.

7. Position the folded ribbon along the folded edge. This is done with all the pages in place to allow for bulk. Pin the ribbon to secure it, and iron in place. (In this project, decorative short lengths of ribbon were placed crosswise under the binding ribbon before it was ironed in place.)

8. Stitch the binding ribbon in place through all page layers, just inside the outer edge of the ribbon. Add an optional line of stitching along the bound edge.

Children love to be alone because alone is where they know themselves, and where they dream.
Roger Rosenblatt

I was never less alone than while by myself. Edward Gibbon

It is easy in the world to live after the world's opinion; it is easy in solitude to live after our own; but the great person is one who in the midst of the crowd keeps with perfect sweetness the independence of solitude. Ralph Waldo Emerson

I often asked if I am not lonely on my solitary excursions. It seems so self-evident that one cannot be lonesome where everything is wild and beautiful and busy and steeped with God that the question is hard to answer. John Muir

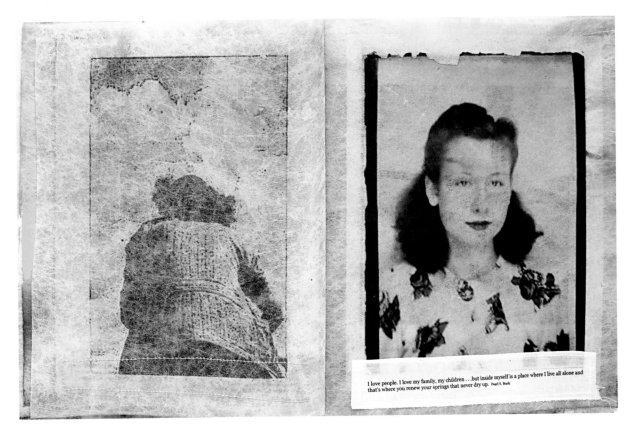

I love people. I love my family, my children . . .but inside myself is a place where I live all alone and that's where you renew your springs that never dry up. Pearl S. Buck

By Lesley Riley

Memento: A Faux Tintype

Materials

Vintage daguerreotype or tintype case or your own case created from cardboard

Black-and-white image printed in reverse on TAP (page 12)

Parchment paper or Silicone Release Paper (Resources, page 63)

Silver-colored craft metal (Project was created with Walnut Hollow aluminum.)

Instructions

See basic transfer instructions (page 13) and TAP on Metal (page 21).

1. Take apart the photo case, and measure the interior. Or create a case or frame to the desired size.

2. Cut the craft metal to size, and check for fit.

3. Transfer the image onto the metal.

4. Reassemble the case, and enjoy!

TAP TIP

If you are starting with a color photo, use photo-editing software to convert a color photo to black and white. For printing the blackest blacks, select Black Ink Only on your printer menu, usually found in the Advanced menu.

I collect vintage daguerreotype and tintype cases for projects like this—using a vintage or modern photo to create an easy faux tintype. Turn your 21st-century friends and family into 19th-century look-alike keepsakes.

By Martina Webb

Finished sizes: various—1⅜" in diameter to 1¼" × 1½"

Technique used: TAP on polymer clay

Polymer Clay Pendants

Materials

Conditioned polymer clay in light or white—Kato or Premo by Sculpey recommended

TAP

Images or photos printed in reverse on TAP (page 12)

Clay cutting tool

Sharpie markers in colors

Small brushes

Decorative craft chalks

Sealing products for polymer clay, such as Varathane and doming resin

Rubber stamps and rubber stamp ink

Isopropyl alcohol

400-grit superfine waterproof sandpaper

Findings
(wire or silver-plated screw eyes)

Superglue

Instructions

See basic transfer instructions (page 13) and TAP on Polymer Clay (page 24).

EIFFEL TOWER PENDANT

1. Color TAP with decorative chalks.

2. Print image in reverse onto TAP over the chalks (page 12).

3. Transfer and bake, following the instructions on page 24.

4. Coat the pendant with Varathane after baking.

SHARPIE PLAID PENDANT

1. Hand draw a plaid pattern with colored Sharpie markers onto TAP.

2. Transfer and bake, following the instructions on page 24.

3. Lightly sand the baked surface to give it a more muted look, like faded fabric.

4. Cover the pendant in doming resin.

VINTAGE GRAPES PENDANT

1. Hand stamp and color in the stamped image on TAP using Sharpie markers and Sharpie "watercolor," created by scribbling the marker onto a metal surface and picking up the ink with an alcohol-wetted paintbrush.

2. Transfer and bake, following the instructions on page 24.

3. Seal as desired after baking.

INKJET ROSE PENDANT

1. Print an image directly on TAP.

2. Transfer and bake, following the instructions on page 24.

3. Seal as desired after baking.

Until now, polymer clay artists have had few foolproof options for transferring images to polymer clay when a bright, photo-quality image is desired. With TAP, endless experimentation and disappointment are eliminated.

Spread Your Wings

By Patty Szymkowicz

Materials

C&T Ready-to-Go Blank Board Book—door shape

Canvas paper (Bienfang Canvasette)

Vintage images and sheet music for front cover, printed in reverse on TAP (page 12)

Parchment paper or Silicone Release Paper (Resources, page 63)

Black brush-tip marker for edging torn image

Map-printed tissue paper

Gold and cream tissue paper

Book text pages

UHU gluestick

Brayer

Ranger Distress Crackle Paint (Picket Fence)

Golden's Transparent Red Iron Oxide

Golden's Liquid Acrylic Quinacridone Burnt Orange

Ranger Adirondack Dye Inks

Brilliance Pigment Inks

Colorbox Stylus

Vintage flower

Krylon Gold Leafing Pen

Vintage velvet ribbon

Golden frill German embellishment

Golden Gel Medium for gluing flower, ribbon, and wings

Butterfly feather wings cut in half

Instructions

See basic transfer instructions (page 13) and TAP on Paper (page 16).

1. Use the gluestick to adhere the tissue paper and music sheet onto the Board Book cover, using a rubber brayer to smooth and help the papers make good contact with the board book.

2. Apply Distress Crackle Paint on the lower portion of the book cover, leaving a bit of room around the edges. When dry, rub with inks, and dry brush with paints.

3. Transfer the vintage image onto the canvas paper. Tear the edges of the image, and color the torn edge with a black brush marker.

4. Glue the transferred image onto gold and cream decorative paper with a layer of netting and with the golden frill tucked in at the bottom. Glue this collage to the book cover.

5. Attach the vintage flower to the cover photo with gel medium.

6. Use a gold Krylon pen around the edges, and attach a strip of velvet ribbon at the bottom with glue.

7. Cut the feather wings in half, and attach them to the back of the Board Book with gel medium, continuing to press them in place as they dry. Add pieces of tissue paper on top of the glued wings, just up to the edge of the back of the book, to help hold them securely in place.

Helen

1929

By Rebekah Meier

Materials

Image and text printed in reverse on TAP (page 12); *Note: Photo should be 3½″ × 5″.*

Parchment paper or Silicone Release Paper (Resources, page 63)

70gm Lutradur cut into 3 pieces—4″ × 6″, 5½″ × 8½″, 2″ × 7″

4″ × 7″ piece of tea-dyed muslin

Paper and fabric scraps

Petal Pink Liquid Rit Dye

Liquid (dropper or bottle) pink and tea color pigment inks

Small cap (from anything)

Rotary cutter with pinking blade

2 embossed batting hearts (page 47)

18-karat gold leaf pen

Small glitter scrapbook brad

Pins

Vintage doily 9″ × 12″ (tea or rust dyed)

2 pieces 14″ × 17½″ of fabric

14″ × 17½″ piece of batting

Seed and pearl beads

Needle (with small eye for beading)

Fabric adhesive

2 pieces of fabric 14″ × 2″ and 2 pieces 17½″ × 2″ for binding

½ yard paper-backed fusible web

Sewing machine and sewing thread

Rebekah's inspiration for this piece comes from a favorite photo of her mother taken when she was five years old. While the photo already has an aged appearance, she loves that she could alter the image with ink dots and puddles before transferring it to Lutradur.

Instructions

See basic transfer instructions (page 13) and TAP on Lutradur (page 18).

1. Fill the dropper with ink, apply dots and puddles onto the TAP-printed image, and let it dry.

2. Apply tea-colored ink onto the rim of a small cap, and stamp onto the printed image.

3. Transfer the printed image onto the 4" × 6" piece of Lutradur.

4. Transfer scrap images left over from previous projects onto the tea-dyed piece of muslin.

5. Transfer the date 1929 to a scrap of Lutradur, and trim it to 1" × 1¾". Machine stitch the printed Lutradur to a fabric scrap.

6. Following the manufacturer's instructions, dye the remaining Lutradur pieces with Petal Pink Rit Dye.

7. Trim the transferred and dyed pieces with a rotary pinking blade.

8. Create embossed batting hearts (at right). Edge the hearts with a gold leaf pen. Layer and secure the hearts with a tiny brad.

9. Refer to the project photo, and layer the fabrics and photo onto the vintage doily. Pin everything in place.

10. Machine stitch the elements.

11. Pin the 2 pieces of 14" × 17½" fabric wrong sides together with the batting between them.

12. Center the collaged doily onto the fabric sandwich, and pin in place.

13. Machine stitch the collaged doily, securing all of the layers together.

14. Sew beads to the quilt.

15. Glue the embossed batting hearts to the front of the quilt with fabric adhesive.

16. Apply fusible web to the wrong side of the binding fabric pieces. With a rotary pinking blade, trim the strips to 1½" wide.

17. Remove the paper backing from the fusible web, wrap the binding around the edges of the quilt, and press, fusing the binding in place. Trim the binding ends even with quilt.

18. Machine topstitch around the binding. Add additional quilting as desired.

EMBOSSED BATTING TECHNIQUE

MATERIALS

Batting (Rebekah used Nature-Fil Bamboo by Fairfield Processing Corporation.)

Textile medium

Doily or lace

Pink and champagne metallic acrylic paint

Spray bottle and water

Parchment paper or Silicone Release Paper (Resources, page 63)

INSTRUCTIONS

1. Cut the batting slightly larger than the lace or doily.

2. Mix 1 part textile medium with 1 part water. Pour the mixture into a spray bottle.

3. Place the batting onto the parchment paper, and mist with the diluted textile medium. The batting should be moist but not saturated.

4. Place the lace or doily onto the misted batting.

5. Cover with parchment or Silicone Release Paper. At this point, the batting and lace or doily should be sandwiched between 2 pieces of parchment or release paper. With an iron set to the cotton setting, press the parchment/release paper, ironing firmly onto the batting. Turn the parchment/release paper and batting over, and press again.

6. Remove the parchment/release paper. Gently pull the lace or doily from the batting to reveal an embossed image. Let it dry.

7. Spray the embossed batting with diluted metallic paint (1 part water to 1 part paint), and let dry.

8. Cut the embossed batting into heart shapes.

A Matter of Perspective

By Judy Coates Perez

Materials

White cotton fabric	Water
Drawing pencil	Embroidery floss
TAP	Batting
Parchment paper or Silicone Release Paper (Resources, page 63)	fast2fuse interfacing
CretaColor AquaStics	Backing fabric
Paintbrush	Sewing machine with free-motion foot (optional)

Instructions

See basic transfer instructions (page 13) and TAP on Fabric (pages 14–15).

1. Create your own line drawing or trace and enlarge the design from the project photo, and scan it into Photoshop or a similar image-editing program. Change the color of the line drawing to a warm gray brown, resize it as desired (page 10), and print it in reverse on TAP (page 12). (The bird and tree image fit on one sheet of TAP, and the sun and landscape portions fit on a second.)

2. With CretaColor soluble crayons, work directly on the printed TAP, to color in the line drawings, and use the paintbrush and water to blend the color. Let it dry.

3. Transfer the painted images to white cotton fabric.

4. Stitch the details with cotton embroidery floss.

5. Layer the stitched fabric over a piece of batting, and add some simple free-motion quilting or hand quilting.

6. Wrap the finished quilt around a piece of fast2fuse to stabilize it.

7. Fuse a piece of fabric to the back.

Betty

By Liz Kettle

Liz's collage work often revolves around story, especially family story. This image is a photo of her grandmother Betty, who loved the beach, tropical flowers, and muumuus. She had quite the collection of muumuus and velvet evening skirts, which she donned with jewels every evening after shedding her business attire. Liz has kept many of those outfits and loves to use them in her collage work.

Materials

Vintage fabrics for quilt front

Batting larger than quilt front fabric

Cotton fabric for backing and binding or facing

Vintage image printed in reverse on TAP (page 12)

Parchment paper or Silicone Release Paper (Resources, page 63)

Hand-dyed silk velvet for collage layer

Rust-dyed silk charmeuse

Pastels, and small paintbrush

Mistyfuse fusible web

Fusible lightweight interfacing or stabilizer

Adhesive water-soluble stabilizer and lightweight water-soluble stabilizer

Heavy cotton thread for hand stitching

Chenille needle for hand stitching

Embellishments: shells, beads, ribbon, plastic veggie netting, silk flowers, silk roving, Angelina fibers, fine tulle, artificial stamens, cellophane flowers, water-soluble stabilizer

Sewing machine and thread for machine stitching, and size 12/80 or 14/90 sharp sewing machine needles

Pins

Instructions

See basic transfer instructions (page 13) and TAP on Fabric (pages 14–15).

1. Cut the vintage fabric to the desired size of the quilt. Layer the fabric with batting and backing. Pin or spray baste, and quilt as desired. Consider using motifs in the fabric for your quilting patterns. Finish the edges with a facing or binding.

2. Tint the vintage photo printed on TAP using pastels. Hard pastels can scratch TAP—instead, use a brush dipped in water to apply the pastel colors. Transfer the tinted image to the rust-dyed silk charmeuse.

3. Fuse the silk charmeuse to the hand-dyed silk velvet. Apply interfacing or stabilizer to the back of the silk to stabilize the fabric for hand stitching.

4. Stitch rice or seed stitches on the charmeuse border around the photo.

5. Make silk flower embellishments (see below).

6. Embroider a feather stitch on the bottom left corner using a variety of threads to suggest seaweed.

7. Stitch on shells, ribbon, silk petals, plastic veggie netting, and silk flowers in corner groupings.

8. Use Mistyfuse to fuse the top collage layer to the quilted base. Press carefully so you do not crush your embellishments.

9. Bead around the perimeter of the collage layer.

SILK FLOWER EMBELLISHMENTS

1. Place a piece of adhesive water-soluble stabilizer on your work surface with the adhesive exposed.

2. Pull out some very fine wisps of silk roving and a tiny amount of Angelina fibers. Place these over the top of the water-soluble stabilizer adhesive. Top with a layer of lightweight water-soluble stabilizer to create a little packet.

3. Draw a couple of different flower designs on top of the water-soluble stabilizer.

4. Place a piece of tulle under the stabilizer packet. Use a hoop if desired. Stitch the layers together using free-motion stitching following the drawn flower design.

5. Trim away excess stabilizer, and rinse the packet under running water to dissolve the stabilizer. Let it dry.

6. Insert artificial stamens or cellophane flowers into the center of the flower, and trim away excess stems. Take a few stitches at the base to cup the flower into a more natural shape.

Poetry Pinafore

By Ruth Rae

When Ruth creates poetry pinafores, she tries to infuse a threadbare, ethereal characteristic in every piece to give them a loved and timeworn appearance. Once the pattern is cut out, beloved words and poems are incorporated onto these dresses. The words are written with free-motion embroidery. The letters are sewn by guiding the fabric under the needle of a sewing machine, much like handwriting.

Materials

Fabric for dress

Small dress pattern of your choice

Photo or image printed in reverse on TAP (page 12)

Parchment paper or Silicone Release Paper (Resources, page 63)

Organza

Lace trim

Sewing machine with free-motion foot

Machine quilting thread

Size 14/90 machine needle

Needle

Pins

Thread

Buttons or other embellishments

Fabric for petticoat (optional)

Embroidery floss and needle (optional)

16-gauge wire and wire cutters (optional)

Instructions

See basic transfer instructions (page 13) and TAP on Fabric (pages 14–15).

1. Cut out the pieces for the dress.

2. Cut out the TAP image, and use your fingernail or something similar to scratch off various parts for a more aged effect (page 25).

3. Cut a piece of organza a little larger than your image. Place the organza on the dress front where you want the transferred image. Place the TAP (image side down) on the organza, and cover with parchment or release paper. Iron to transfer. The image will be transferred onto the organza, and there will be a shadow effect on the dress front.

4. Pin the organza on the shadow layer on the dress, and sew over it in a decorative fashion.

5. Attach the free-motion foot to your sewing machine, and put the feed dogs into the down position. Place the front of the dress under the sewing foot, and guide the fabric under the needle, using it as you would a pencil, writing the words of your choice onto the piece.

6. Make the dress.

OPTIONAL STEPS

- After the dress is complete, make a lace petticoat to go underneath it. More details can be added by adding hand stitching and gathering stitches to help add the suggestion of movement to your piece.

- Make a hanger for your clothes with 14″ of 16-gauge wire. Bend the wire into a hanger and you can now hang your *Poetry Pinafore* on its own hanger!

Grace

By Theresa Martin

Various fabrics, vintage lace, a transparency, and patinaed copper were sewn together to frame the TAP transfer image of a little girl. The girl was scanned from a vintage CDV (Carte de Visite) and was colored in Photoshop prior to printing.

Materials

Large piece of fabric for collage base

Photo printed in reverse on TAP (page 12)

Parchment paper or Silicone Release Paper
(Resources, page 63)

Various fabric scraps

Vintage lace

Paper ephemera

Transparency with printed image

Patinaed copper (behind image)

Ribbon, embellishments

Sewing machine (optional) and thread

Instructions

*See basic transfer instructions (page 13)
and TAP on Fabric (pages 14–15).*

1. Transfer the TAP image onto a piece of fabric.

2. Select coordinating fabrics, laces, papers, and mixed
media to create a collage with the image as the focal point.
Pin all the elements in place when you are happy with the
arrangement.

3. Stitch the collage in place by hand or machine.

Abelha

By Jane Dávila

Materials

White prewashed or PFD (prepared for dyeing) fabric

Image printed in reverse on TAP (page 12)

Parchment paper or Silicone Release Paper (Resources, page 63)

Acrylic ink

Fabric medium

Foam brushes

fast2fuse interfacing

Small pieces of commercial fabric

Commercial or handmade stamps (Chunky designs, as opposed to finely detailed designs, work better.)

Small strip of paper with interesting texture at least 10″ long (Jane used a mesh Maruyama paper from Magenta.)

Linen or cotton embroidery floss and hand sewing needle

Acrylic paint and a small paintbrush

Threads to match and contrast with fabrics

Sewing machine

Makeup/cosmetic sponge

Instructions

See basic transfer instructions (page 13) and TAP on Fabric (pages 14–15).

1. Dilute acrylic ink with water in a small plastic container. More water to ink will result in paler colors than less water to ink. Using a foam brush, apply to the white fabric. For neat light and dark effects, crumple the fabric slightly, and then set it aside to dry. Make several colored pieces for the quilt—Jane made a teal blue (about 14″ × 10″) and a light olive (about 7″ × 6″).

2. Cut a piece of one of your lighter fabrics 6″ × 5¼″, and transfer the image onto this fabric.

3. Cut a piece of fabric for the quilt background approximately 9¼″ × 9¼″. Cut a piece of fast2fuse interfacing and a piece of commercial fabric (to use as a backing) the same size as the background.

4. Fuse the background fabric to the fast2fuse interfacing. Using the design of your choice, free-motion machine quilt all over the background. Because the image is a bee, Jane used a hexagon shape as a quilting motif. Fuse the backing fabric in place now.

5. Cut a strip of background fabric 3½″ × 9¼″. Flip it over. It should be lighter on the opposite side. Mix a very small amount of acrylic ink into a little bit of fabric medium. Using a foam brush, apply the medium/ink mixture to a handmade or commercial stamp, and stamp it all over the strip of fabric. Using more medium than ink will result in a translucent effect. Set aside to dry.

6. Cut a strip of interesting paper 1″ × 9¼″. Cut a piece of commercial fabric 1½″ × 2½″. Lay all of the fabric and paper pieces, including the transferred image and the stamped strip,

into position on the background fabric (refer to the photo for placement). Sew each piece into place, through all the layers. Consider using decorative stitches such as a blanket stitch or feather stitch, as well as a straight stitch.

7. Trim the quilt to 9″ × 9″. Sew multiple rows of parallel straight stitching around the perimeter of the quilt. Dilute a very small amount of ink with fabric medium, and using a makeup/cosmetic sponge, very lightly and sparingly apply to the perimeter of the quilt to provide a subtle darkening of the edge.

8. Using linen or cotton embroidery floss, sew a few random hand stitches here and there around the quilt.

New Moon Dolls

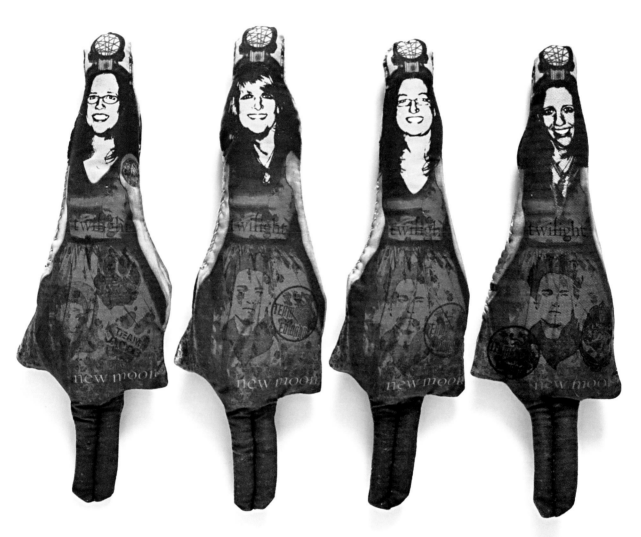

By Michelle I. Tompkins

Michelle created these dolls as a gift for her friends when they attended *The Twilight Saga: New Moon* premiere. She says, "It's really fun to show up at a theater full of 500 women and have them offer you tons of money to make them a *Twilight* doll, to scream with fun and happiness with the joy of seeing a fun movie, and to experience the pure joy of being with girlfriends and making crafts!"

Finished size: 3" × 7" (each)

Technique used: TAP on fabric

Materials

Full-length photo(s) of friends or family

TAP

Parchment paper or Silicone Release Paper
(Resources, page 63)

Fabric for transfers

Polyfil or cotton stuffing

Needle and coordinating thread

Photo-editing software (optional)

It helps if you are computer savvy, because a lot
of the work for the dolls in this project was done
in Photoshop. You can substitute hand drawing or
coloring directly on TAP prior to transfer for most
of the Photoshop actions. Just remember, all text
needs to be done in reverse if you are doing it by
hand. Many great books on digital scrapbooking and
mixed-media digital work exist today to assist you
in using Photoshop, Photoshop Elements, or other
photo-editing software for these types of projects.
(See Resources on page 63.)

Instructions

*See basic transfer instructions (page 13) and TAP on Fabric
(pages 14–15).*

1. Design the doll front and back either by hand or by
using a digital photo and photo-editing software (at right).
Alternatively, you can skip the back design and use a coordinating fabric instead.

2. The back of the doll needs to be the exact reverse of the
front so that they match up perfectly when sewn together.
Use the front as a pattern. If you want to use a photograph
as the back of the doll, it will take some adjusting to be an
exact fit—this is best left to those familiar with Photoshop.
Using coordinated fabric is faster and much easier.

3. Print a sample on paper, and verify all the details. Print the
final image in reverse on TAP, and iron to transfer onto the
fabric.

4. After transferring, you can further embellish with stamps,
stitching, rhinestones, and more before sewing the doll
together.

5. Place the doll pieces right sides together, and machine or
hand-stitch the front and back together, leaving an opening
large enough to turn the doll inside out. Turn and stuff the
doll with Polyfil. Hand stitch closed.

Designing Your Doll with Photo-Editing Software

① Use a digital camera to take a full-length front
and rear photo of the person or people you are
making into a doll.

② In Photoshop or a similar photo-editing program, use editing and filters to create the look you
desire. Michelle used the *Bitmap* and *Graphic Pen*
filters to create the sketchy graphic pencil effect
that looks like she sketched in pen and ink.

③ Add a crown if desired—Michelle took a photo
of a throne, cropped it to make it into a crown, and
placed it on the doll's head. She also styled the
hair using Photoshop's *Brush* tools.

④ Add decorative details by scanning other
images, or use text. By creating with layers in
Photoshop, you can move details around or delete
them as desired. When you are satisfied with your
image, flatten the layers in preparation for printing.
Reverse the image for transfer.

Treasure Box/ Shkatulochka

By Natalya Aikens

Doing the laundry is no longer a chore when you are creating art supplies. Natalya has created a beautiful gift box using recycled dryer sheets and dryer lint.

Materials

Used gift box with sturdy sides
(A colored box is best.)

Photo of an architectural element

Photo-editing software, such as
Photoshop or Photoshop Elements

TAP

Parchment paper or Silicone Release
Paper (Resources, page 63)

Used dryer sheets

A bit of dryer lint

Tulle or netting a bit larger
than box top

Acrylic paints

Foam brush

Water-based glue
(Matte medium is perfect.)

Fabric at least as large as the box

Detail scissors or craft knife and
cutting mat

Decorative threads and
hand sewing needle

Sewing machine (optional)

Instructions

*See basic transfer instructions (page 13)
and TAP on Lutradur (page 18).*

1. Cut used dryer sheets into 9 squares
to make a Nine-Patch block. Make sure
the finished block will measure larger
than the top of the box by about ¼″ to
½″. Sew the seams, and press them flat.

2. Wet the quilt block, and paint it
with diluted acrylic paint to achieve
a transparent look. Natalya used a
magenta color and then added gold
in a few spots for a shimmery effect.
Allow it to dry completely before transferring the image.

3. Choose images from your photos
that are clear and sharp. Unless you are
a whiz at Photoshop, it is easiest to use
a dark image on a light background.
Natalya loves the look of ornate

wrought iron fences; for this purpose,
she photographed them against the
sky to get the clearest images. Crop
and size the images to your liking (page
10), keeping the dryer sheet Nine-Patch
in mind for the sizes. The *Stamp* filter
in Photoshop gave the images the look
of rubber stamps.

4. Open a new document in your
photo program. Drag your stamp
images to this new document,
rotating them as desired using the *Free
Transform* option. Natalya arranged the
images to mimic the Nine-Patch block.
Print your images in a few different
sizes on plain copy paper to help figure
out which size will work best for your
purposes.

Alternatives to using photo-
editing software are to draw
designs directly on TAP or
to copy appropriately sized
designs on TAP and transfer
them separately.

5. When you have figured out the correct size, print the images in reverse on TAP (page 12). Cut away the white areas as closely as possible. You can color any remaining white areas with a colored pencil or a marker to match your painted dryer sheet Nine-Patch. Another option is to scratch away areas of the image to make it less perfect or to feather out some areas. When you are satisfied with the TAP image, transfer it to the dryer sheet Nine-Patch.

6. Cut a piece of tulle or netting slightly larger than the Nine-Patch. To create the raised center square, take a small square of color-coordinated dryer lint (or batting), and place it behind the square. Complete the quilt sandwich by placing and pinning the netting in place over the dryer lint and the whole square. Use free-motion stitching or hand-stitching to attach the netting to the Nine-Patch. Add beads or additional embellishments as desired.

7. To finish the outer sides of the box top, cut strips of coordinating fabric the width of the box sides, and glue them on, overlapping at the edges. Lightly brush glue along the upper and lower edges of the sides to prevent raveling.

8. Put glue on the back of the dryer lint portion of the Nine-Patch, and center it on the box lid, gluing into place. With a contrasting and thicker thread and hand stitch the Nine-Patch to the lid through the cardboard. Figure out where the stitches will make the best impact without worrying about the stitches in the box lid; they will be covered later. You can also glue the entire Nine-Patch to the box top, but the glue will harden the delicate dryer sheets. Fusing is another option.

9. Measure the inside of the box lid (do not include the sides). Choose a fabric to line the inside of the box top and cover your stitching. Cut the fabric slightly larger than the inside measurement. Glue the trimmed square inside the lid, covering up the stitches and needle holes. As an option, brush glue or matte medium on the wrong side of the fabric and let dry before cutting. This will make cutting the correct size easier and less likely to fray.

Resources

Most of the products used in this book can be found at your local or online craft or quilt store. It helps to Google an item so you know what you are looking for when you go shopping. Items that are harder to find are listed below.

TAP, Lutradur, and Silicone Release Paper are available at quilt and craft stores or at www.ctpub.com.

DIGITAL COLLAGE/QUILTING BOOKS

Digital Expressions: Creating Digital Art with Adobe Photoshop Elements, by Susan Tuttle. North Light Books, 2010.

Paper + Pixels: Scrapbook Layouts, by Mary Flaum and Audrey Neal. Memory Makers Books, 2008.

Secrets of Digital Quilting—From Camera to Quilt, by Lura Schwarz Smith and Kerby C. Smith. C&T Publishing, 2010.

SPECIALTY PRODUCTS

Acrylic paints, inks, and mediums: Liquitex Surface Design Center at local quilt and craft stores or local art stores

Copper Mesh: www.RandomArtsNow.com

Craft Metal: Local craft stores or www.WalnutHollow.com

Mica: www.VolcanoArts.com

Non-steaming iron: Vermont Country Store (www.vermontcountrystore.com)

Ready-to-Go Blank Board Books: Local craft stores or www.ctpub.com

Resin for polymer: www.deco-coat.com/uv.html or www.objectsandelements.com

Twilight stamps: 8 Assorted Rubber Stamps with Ink Pad by Summit Entertainment

Wood products: Local craft stores or www.WalnutHollow.com

CONTRIBUTING ARTISTS

Natalya Aikens: ArtbyNatalya.com

Jane Dávila: JaneDavila.com

Liz Kettle: TextileEvolution.com

Theresa Martin: TheresaMartin.com

Rebekah Meier: RebekahMeier.net

Judy Coates Perez: JudyPerez.blogspot.com

Nina Perez: NinaFPerez.blogspot.com

Ruth Rae: RuthRae.com

Patty Szymkowicz: bitze.wordpress.com

Michelle I. Tompkins: vindicatedstudios.com

Martina Webb: etsy.com/shop/BlossomArts

About the Author

First known for her Fragment series of small fabric collages, Lesley is now an internationally known art quilter and mixed-media artist with a passion for photos, color, and the written word. She has taught extensively in the United States and as far away as Italy and Australia. Her art and articles have appeared in numerous publications and juried shows. Her first book, *Quilted Memories*, brought new ideas and techniques to quilting and preserving memories. Lesley's second book, *Fabric Memory Books*, combines fabric and innovative ideas with the art of book-making. *Fabulous Fabric Art with Lutradur* (C&T) takes a new material to a new level. Lesley defines Lutradur as "the magic in the middle"—an art material that combines the best properties of both fabric and paper.

Lesley has filmed three instructional DVDs with Creative Catalyst Productions and Interweave. Not one to be camera shy, Lesley has also appeared on three episodes of *Quilting Arts* television, Season 1. Currently, Lesley is the host of Blog Talk Radio's *Art & Soul* show.

Realizing that artists, both new and experienced, often need more than new ideas and techniques to fulfill their art dreams, Lesley started Artist Success, where she shares her experience and knowledge as a coach and mentor, providing solutions for the struggling artist. For more information and free articles and solutions, visit ArtistSuccess.com.

When not coaching, teaching, writing about, or making art, Lesley, a Washington, D.C., native, loves spending time with her husband, six children, and six granddaughters.

For more information about her art and classes, visit Lesley's website, LesleyRiley.com.

Previous books by Lesley Riley:

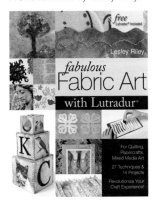

Great Titles *from* C&T PUBLISHING

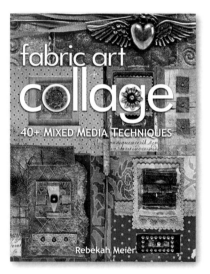

Available at your local retailer or **www.ctpub.com** *or* **800-284-1114**

For a list of other fine books from C&T Publishing, visit our website to view our catalog online

C&T PUBLISHING, INC.

P.O. Box 1456
Lafayette, CA 94549
800-284-1114

Email: ctinfo@ctpub.com
Website: www.ctpub.com

C&T Publishing's professional photography services are now available to the public. Visit us at www.ctmediaservices.com.

Tips and Techniques can be found at www.ctpub.com > Consumer Resources > Quiltmaking Basics: Tips & Techniques for Quiltmaking & More

For quilting supplies:

COTTON PATCH

1025 Brown Ave.
Lafayette, CA 94549
Store: 925-284-1177
Mail order: 925-283-7883

Email: CottonPa@aol.com
Website: www.quiltusa.com

Note: Fabrics used in the quilts shown may not be currently available, as fabric manufacturers keep most fabrics in print for only a short time.